THE WIND STILLS TO LISTEN

Deirdre Cartmill

THE WIND STILLS TO LISTEN

ARLEN HOUSE

The Wind Stills to Listen

is published in 2023 by
ARLEN HOUSE
42 Grange Abbey Road
Baldoyle
Dublin D13 A0F3
Ireland
Email: arlenhouse@gmail.com
www.arlenhouse.ie

ISBN 978–1–85132–307–4, paperback

International distribution
SYRACUSE UNIVERSITY PRESS
621 Skytop Road, Suite 110
Syracuse
New York 13244–5290
USA
Email: supress@syr.edu
www.syracuseuniversitypress.syr.edu

© Deirdre Cartmill, 2023

The moral right of the author has been asserted

Typesetting by Arlen House

Front cover image by Steve Johnson
Back cover image 'Cavehill Belfast' by Orlagh Finnegan

Contents

7   *Acknowledgements*

Torn Green Blanket
13   Between Crossing and Passing
15   They Are All Bridges of the Dead
16   Torn
18   Signs of Life
21   Daily Bread
22   When Do I Die?
23   The Dead in the Earth
24   Crossing Points

The Museum of Broken Relationships
29   The Museum of Broken Relationships
30   Flower Moon
31   Fishmarket Pas de Deux
33   Aurora
34   Seed
35   Desire Path
36   The Gathering
37   Blossom
38   Intercession

41   *Until the Wind Stops Singing*

82   *About the Author*

Acknowledgements

Thank you to the editors of the following where some of these poems, or earlier versions of them, were previously published or broadcast: *Abridged; FourXFour; Her Other Language: Women Writers from the North of Ireland Address Abuse and Domestic Violence* (Arlen House); *Honest Ulsterman; Poetry Ireland Review* and *Reading the Future: New Writing from Ireland* (Arlen House). 'Between Crossing and Passing' was included on Ireland's Poetry Jukebox 'A Deeper Country' curation in 2019. 'Torn' was included on *One Minute Poems* – an audio anthology from Rancid Idol Productions for Poetry Day UK 2022.

'Crossing Points' was created during my time as the Irish Writers Centre Roaming Writer–in–Residence 2019. It was recorded and shared online as an audio journey that passengers could listen to in situ while travelling.

Some of these poems were birthed during a residency at An Creagan. 'The Museum of Broken Relationships' was written after visiting the museum of the same name in Zagreb, Croatia.

Other poems in this collection were inspired by my time travelling across Europe, devising and showcasing *Bridging the Silence* as part of the Corners European project. *Bridging the Silence* is an audio walk and installation shown on pedestrian bridges that tells the stories of survivors of domestic abuse, sexual abuse, political violence and transgender issues. The audio walk mixes my poetic narration with real life testimonies, sounds and music. I created this installation alongside Hrvoslava Brkušić, Croatian multimedia and sound artist, and Beatriz Churruca, a Basque visual artist and performer. It premiered at the Belfast International Arts Festival in October 2015. It then toured Europe and was presented in Blyth, England; Zagreb, Croatia; Ljubljana, Slovenia; Gdansk, Poland and in San Sebastian, the Basque Country as part of the City of Culture events. I am grateful to Corners and the Arts Council of Northern Ireland for funding and supporting this work.

Thank you to ACNI for SIAP awards which allowed me to work on this collection. Many thanks to Damian Gorman for feedback, and Lucy Caldwell and Moyra Donaldson for kind endorsements. I also want to thank my partner Robert, my siblings Darragh, Sinead, Aisling and Orlagh, and my friends Celine, Samantha and Michelle for their love and support, and for always believing in me.

THE WIND STILLS TO LISTEN

TORN GREEN BLANKET

Between Crossing and Passing

A ghost is a whisper
that yearns to cross over
from that world to this,

and we walk with these whispering souls
with only their stories to bear witness,

and when they're not welcomed,
when they're not heard,
they will force their way over.

They will take to the water
or stride in the air,
suspended between heaven and here,

and at that halfway point
neither in that world nor this

they will stay, wait, touch the hair
of someone who passes,
slip a hand in a pocket,
breathe on a neck,

anything to sate that unmet need
to be seen, heard,
to know their journey was worth it,

and to keep their story breathing
they will whisper

remember
my body in the sand,
my schoolbag in the rubble,
my face under water,

and they will keep whispering
see me, hear me,
until we reach back
and hold them as they tremble

between dead and undead,
between crossing and passing.

They Are All Bridges of the Dead

where derelict factories and coal docks stand guard
over dog shit and broken bottles,

where people pass over
to go to the market or race for the last tram,

but there is always that pushback
from bodies putrefying in the water.

It slips into the rust and graffiti,
is lost in the floods, leaks back,

and not even the swoop and glide of the swans
before they crash-land in a thunderous spray

can mask the unrelenting flow
of blood still spilling,

of life rotting in a river bed.

Torn

I see you crying at the gate,
and I am back at another gate

where you hoisted me on your shoulders

and the horn of the hunt
quivered through the fields,

and I saw the horses race
but I didn't see the hare,

blood pulsing

as its hind legs flexed
to bolt, zigzag, leap,

and I didn't see the hounds' teeth
rip into its neck,

then trail its dripping entrails

back to their masters
to blood their young,

and as I watch you weep
I still don't see

what lies beneath the hedge line

– the blood stains on your shirt,
the debris on your tongue,

because I didn't see what you saw,
the ripped limbs flung across the street,

the dead eyes open,

and the wee one floating in the water
in a torn green blanket.

Signs of Life

The Test

The blue cross rises from the white,
like a photograph emerging from a negative
and slowly filling with the possibility of life.

My hand quivers like a brushed string
vibrating to its own low hum,
yearning to release its first song.

I pass him this miracle
and my gift becomes our secret,
as we mark off each day until we'll hold you.

We search online, try to gauge your size
– a coffee bean, a walnut, sprouting buds
that will become limbs as the days go by.

But when we hand you to the doctor
and she scans you for the first time,
you disappear like a film exposed to light.

Skin

I sink the blade into my fleshy forearm.
I need to mark your presence on my skin.

It's been four weeks but their words still make me flinch
when they coo 'you'll have another child soon.'

I'm afraid to sleep because the nightmares come.
They snatch you from my grip again and again,

and I wake alone, with nothing but a cold sweat
and a steel blade to tame my fickle flesh.

First Steps

It's knowing that what I imagined will never be
– tickling your tummy, pushing you on the swings,
teaching you to build sandcastles on the beach.

You're a kite pulled free by the wind
and I find myself following you, playing catch up,
hoping that I'll rejoin you at the road's end,

when I will finally cross the distance between us
and you will be waiting to coax me towards you.
You'll take my hand as I take my first steps

into your arms, one again becoming two,
and you will mother me as I would have mothered you.

Daily Bread

I can't let go of this image of you,
scavenging through a dump for food,
then toddling away and bum-crawling into
a grain bag to settle down to sleep.

You don't remember your mother singing
as you rested your head on her back.
Wrapped in cotton and moving in tandem
you fell asleep as her fever grew.

You only know this dump, this path,
the feet passing by, the hunger inside,
this dirty dress, these bare feet.

As I scrape my leftovers into the bin,
you lift a piece of half-eaten bread,
pick the mould off, chew it slowly,

chase a rat as you wait for the next truck,
and I watch and wait, and do nothing. Nothing.

When Do I Die?

When my last breath
stutters from my lungs
and my thready pulse
gives up its fragile dance?

Or when the doctor condemns me
with a looming end date,
and I am chained to a monitor
that beep-counts my slow decay?

Or each time my heart contracts
and blocks the flow of blood
for a sliver of a second
like another small death?

Or when my heart relaxes
and another second passes
with another wasted breath
as I dither and do nothing?

And if so, when do I live?

The Dead in the Earth

Holub made me think
about the dead in the earth,

of how there are more of them than us,
of how we walk on their faces.

But one day we must merge
with those other earth dwellers

in a way we couldn't do in life,
when our bodies decompose

and our skin, muscles, cells
slough off and decay,

forming minerals that feed the earth
as we once fed off it;

and in that perfect symmetry
we are rats on a wheel

repeating and repeating,
still thinking we have choices.

Crossing Points

Coal black sky. No moon.
I journey into the dark.
Which me will emerge?

*

Like a tree growing
towards the sun, half blossom,
half stunted, two-faced.

*

The horizon shrinks
to the edge of the fog. Lost,
seeking colour, light.

*

Clickety-clack whoosh,
this eternal drive forward.
Where are we going?

*

We change direction,
like points levered left to right,
set on a new path.

*

The signal turns green.
The brakes come off. Everything
seems possible now.

*

Keep back from the edge.
You might leap off, spread your arms
and fly, born to it.

*

Abandoned things – sheds,
trains, a windowless cottage,
broken glass, scrapped dreams.

*

Things can be reborn.
A rusting car in a field
now a nesting place.

*

Derelict watchtowers
where the slumbering border
wakes. Pray and hold tight.

*

Swans on a grey lake.
Rain slicks sleeting the windows.
A torn sky weeping.

*

Window reflections.
Me superimposed on you,
joined without touching.

*

Moving through shadow,
crossing from sun into rain,
life in light and shade.

*

Angel wings in clouds
lift my gaze upwards, guide me
home. Will I follow?

THE MUSEUM OF BROKEN RELATIONSHIPS

The Museum of Broken Relationships

Love is a lie in a promise,
but oh that moment when all seems possible,
that teasing glimpse of more

when I synch my breath to yours
and my heart slows to your rhythm,
and this is the first loss.

Do I love you,
or the places where our wounds touch
and the ache is just enough

to wake us from our numbness?
We are like pages joined by a perforated edge
and how little it takes to tear them apart,

but the dreamer can't stop dreaming,
so I step into the labyrinth,
its exit lost or forgotten,

the water flooding in and rising
as I set out on that first stroke,
knowing I will drown.

Flower Moon

The cherry blossom drops its petals
and a cobweb spun across a white rose

catches the sun, weaves the petals
into a half-open doorway

where the petals fold into a womb,
and what magic might be birthed

if you come and dance with me
under the flower moon?

Fishmarket Pas de Deux

He slaps an octopus awake
in this place of suffocation.
I protest by not entering,
partake by watching.

She walks backwards with a mirror
past crates of oranges with green leaves
and white fish splayed in plastic trays.
Her polka-dot sneakers trail through the sand.

She turns to the sea, walks to the edge.
Her black gloved hands pluck at her ears
and the wind ripples her t-shirt,
manic against her stillness.

Now she sees him scooping up shellfish.
She steps closer, gently invasive,
strokes the back of her head with her finger.
Her yellow scarf is a kite in the wind.

He glances up. She walks to his side.
His eyes follow in a silent dance,
until his eyes meet hers;
they exchange a few words.

She turns to another
who shouts *quattro, quattro,*
but still her eyes are on him.
She draws him in

until he waves his hand in the air
and goes back to his work, smiling.
The smoke from the chimneys across the bay
fills their lungs like an incoming tide,

and yet they choose to stay,
and the dance below goes on,
and when I look up
they both stand beside me.

Her scarf has turned purple.
He gives me an orange,
and a broken black net
tied to the railing below me

flutters like a lover's ribbon.

Aurora

It's not the snow that makes me cold.
It's the dark with no let-up.

The blackness has consumed the stars
and the moonlight barely breaks
the emptiness.

A trail of pawprints
leads nowhere,

yet I know the rising sun
will lay this dark to rest,
set flame to the horizon,

and when night calls the shadows back,
and your spirit dances across the sky,

I will rise to meet you,

and somewhere in the crossing over
between the high moon and the low sun

I will become the morning star.

Seed

A fire burns in the dark.
Ash falls on my face, my hair.

I lie in the heat of the embers
and feel the pull of the earth,

as if my body wants to sprout roots
and bed into the darkness.

I am a seed that yearns to crack open,
the first hint of life,

the promise of rebirth,
waiting for the dawn's awakening light.

Desire Path

The quickest way from here to there
is always through the weeds and nettles,
the thickened hedges, the overhanging branches
pushed aside to let the sun dip in.

The erosion of what's gone before
reveals the untouched substrata,
the soft earth, the seeds buried for too long
that always wanted to reach up.

The Gathering

Like starlings gathering at dusk
you call me to you,

until every lost part of me
is whirling as one;

you gather me in your arms
and I murmur *home*.

Blossom

Lying lost and crying
under the apple blossom,

when the wind lifts
and blossoms fall down on me,

and I know love as a miracle,
focused in a petal

caught in my palm,
skin thin.

INTERCESSION

Silver confetti blows into the gutter,
ready to shred in the next rain.

The sky sparks with a flash of silver
as a seagull turns on the wind.

I slip into the hospital chapel
where St Filomena smiles down on the old

who stay to kneel and venerate
after the young have left to dance, forget.

I pass through each Station of the Cross,
dig my fingernails into my heart,

and I don't know if it's to release old blood
or to shock it back into love.

Sun flares through a stained-glass window.
I rise into its warmth,

and let the reflection of Christ
wash over my upturned face.

Until the Wind Stops Singing

Until the Wind Stops Singing
Mary Magdalene

I

I follow in the footsteps of my love,

scrabble and claw through the mob,
screaming 'I'm here', but the blood

floods his eyes, nose, mouth
and blinds him, chokes him,

and the wounds in his back ooze open
as the wood rips off more skin.

He falls again.

I scutter forward on my knees,
take his face in my hands,

mop up his blood with my veil.
Is this the last time I will hold him?

A soldier punches me in the gut.
I fall into the dirt.

The soldier kicks him in the ribs
and commands him to get up.

He tries to rise; his knees buckle
but the soldier whips him until he stands,

and I scramble along by his side,
reaching out, unable to touch,

but my eyes never leave his,
and his eyes never leave mine.

His bloodied eyes never leave mine.

II

Did I know when I first saw him?
I'd heard the rumours of course,
the whisperings of Messiah, healer.
I close my eyes and I'm back on that shore.

He sits on the sand as I knot the nets,
and those who follow gather around him.
His voice is a song on the wind
and my heart sings back.

I edge closer with each knot.
He weaves words as I weave nets,
and as these nets capture musht and biny,
his words capture the hearts that listen,

and though I don't want to follow
I am drawn by the pull,
as something in him calls to me
to step forward into ... what?

My feet move towards him
and with each step in the sand
I leave my home behind
and find my home in him.

III

He rises from the water,
and I know I should turn away

but I watch each muscle flex
as he stands, eyes closed,
and turns his face to the sun.

My fingers yearn to follow
the sculpted flow of his back.

He sinks down, rises again,
hair pinned against his skin,

and still his body rises.
I trace each curve and crevice,
each distant island,

and too late I realise
his eyes trace me back.

I turn and run, hear his thighs
push through the water,

parting the sea,
and as he steps ashore I stop,

wanting to run on,
wanting to turn back.

IV

He fingers the edge of his sleeve,
then lifts a box from the folds of his tunic.

'For you,' he says
– so many words for others,
so quiet with me.

A heart is carved on the lid.
'All I have to give,' he says.
All I need, I think,
but the words won't come.

He lets his fingers fall on my neck,
pulls me close, his beard
tickling my nose, my lips.

My mouth opens,
his tongue finds mine
and they circle in a dance
and his breath flows into me
and mine into him,
and we breathe as one,

and when our tongues stop their dance
and our lips part,
we still breathe as one.

I slip the box inside my simlāh
and vow to carry his heart with me.

V

Abba, Father, tell me,
is this what you ask of me,

to walk with him
though I know not where he goes?

Is he the one whose soul
knows the journey as my own?

I have always been your servant.
I have always felt your love,

but this love tears at me.
Take this fear from my belly.

Let me know you walk with us.
Tell me he will lead me back to you.

VI

'Blessed are the poor in spirit.'
He pauses to hear God's whisper,
and a hundred souls hold their breath.

It's as if his eyes see every one,
and then those eyes fall on me,
as my body is stripped away
and only my soul stands before him.

'Master,' I ask, 'what must I do to be blessed?'
He answers, though I don't hear the words.

I only see the sun lighting his eyes
and the skin flaking from his lips,
but I know I have played my part

and I will ask him again
when he takes my hand
and teaches me down by the water.

VII

As the lame man walks
a priest leaps from the crowd,
grips his wrist and screams
'blasphemer,
this is the devil's work.'

John pulls the priest away,
still shouting 'tell me your name, demon.'

The crowd crushes in
like vultures around fresh carrion,
screeching as if to wake the dead.

*

Why don't they see what I see?
Each time he lays his hands

I see the love flow,
and it's this love that makes them whole;

this easing of their heart
eases their disease, unites body and soul.

I feel this love from God
every time he touches me,

and I hope he feels this love
flow from me to him

when I hold him in the dark,
ease his pain of seeing all,

of knowing too much
and feeling too intensely,

and I hope he knows
that if he falls

I will lift him back up
to be healed and made whole.

VIII

I grind some cinnamon,
mix it with oil and myrrh,
make spirals with my finger
as I swirl it in.

I dribble the oil over wet clay,
stretch and shape it
until the oil and clay are one.

I lay the poultice on his bruised wrist,
wrap it in cotton,
lost in the work

until his fingers touch mine
and trace a line
down the side of my hand.

I look up, don't realise
he is pulling me close
until our lips touch
and my body shudders

and his hand is on my waist
and the dropped clay
stains my tunic.

IX

Shadow flames dance on my face
but the heat does not reach
where I lie among fallen figs.

I burst a pod, let the flesh
slide down my hands, soft
as his oil rubbed wrist
slipping through my wet fingers.

Someone moves from the fire
and I pray it is him.
He whispers my name.
I forget to breathe.

He lies down behind me.
His arm slides around my waist
and his hand finds mine,
and our fingers entwine like acacia roots.

I sink back into him
like a stone into water,
but I know I will not sleep.

X

I stand in the waves, waiting for him.
The spray skims my skin
like the brush of a wingtip

then his arms slip around me,
his hands are on my belly
and his breath lifts each hair on my neck.

He pulls me under
and as my head arches back
salt dances on my tongue

and as we rise again
he kisses me,
and I pray we can stay,

but even as I ask it
he leads me ashore,
and I kneel and knead his feet

as he tells me what God
has shown him today,
and I share my visions from God,

and we tease out the meaning
as I tease out his muscles,
and it's as if God is guiding my hands,

and he falls silent
as God joins us as one.

XI

Abba, Father, let me love my love
with the love you give me,

and though you carry him on this earth,
let me also carry him

in my prayers, in my caress.
Let me be a child of the light,

with my beloved holding me
as I hold him, always in the light.

XII

I kneel in the cave,
moonlight at its mouth,
the darkness soft around me

and I open my heart to God.
Peace rises within me
and I feel God there,

for God is this peace.

I sink deeper into my heart
and my soul is touched by God,

and my soul is God,

and yet my soul yearns
to journey home to God.

But what if I can learn
to hold God in my heart,
to let him speak through me

and act through me,
so I can be with God now?

XIII

I watch her hunkering at a distance,
straining to hear his words.

As I go to her, she rises, cries *unclean*,
but her toeless feet don't carry her far.

I can't heal her as he can,
but I can lay my hands and share God's love

and remind her, her body may waste
but her soul is pure and unending,

and will one day rise back to God.

XIV

I wish I'd known him as a child.
We would have walked the shores
in search of magic,
and swam at night
under the stars.

Now we've found the magic
of God in our hearts,
but these bodies feel the ache
of every stone cutting through worn sandals,
every thorn prick drawing blood.

Still we push forward
to unknown faces,
to those who may listen
and those who may not,
to those who may spit on us,

but we let the words settle in their hearts
like sprinkled seeds, waiting
for the right coming together
of sun and rain and damp earth
to burst forth.

We shine a light in the darkness
and leave a flicker behind,
a star to guide them
on their path back home
to their own hearts.

XV

The moon scythes the sky
and gathers us together,

and they ask me to teach,
say he can't understand
the pull on our wombs,
the pain of birth,
the power forced down,
the words held back.

So I speak of all God has told us,
of how God gave birth to us
as we give birth to men
who shun us, break us, rape us

– yet we do not stop giving birth,
and with each birth we hope this newborn
will live the love it has been born in,
just as God hopes with each birth.

And just as we love and forgive
no matter what our children do to us,
so does God love and forgive us,
for we are all His sons and daughters

and He loves each one of us,
and He does not love one more than another,

whether first born or last born,
lowborn or highborn,
whether shepherd, carpenter, priest, mother,
for He does not care what we do with our hands.

We are born of God's heartlove
and He reads our hearts
and with our hearts we praise Him
and with our hearts we love Him
and with our hearts we hear Him speak to us
and all are one in love.

I speak of how we must
find God within us,
that no other can do that for us,

that God will not deny our approach,
but like a loving mother
will welcome us back into His heartlove,
as He wants us to dance in His love.

But first we must love ourselves
with that mother's love,

and remember the moon rises
just as the sun rises,
and both are needed
and neither is more important than the other.

XVI

'Just let me hold you,' I say.
'Let all go for a moment.'

He softens into my belly,
and I stroke his head, feel the tears come.

As sure as a nursing mother
holds their baby, skin on skin,

responds to each tiny movement,
so he responds to me.

I already know he is only half mine,
that he belongs with our Father,

and that he will return home
much sooner than I want him to

and I must let go.

But for now he is mine,
curled in my arms like a newborn,

and I will hold this moment
when that other moment comes,

and when I can no longer hold him,
I will carry him within me.

But for now we must let the pain flow,
and after we will walk together in the sun

like children, laughing for no reason,
with no thought of what's to come.

XVII

Abba, Father, guide me.
Let me do what you ask of me.

Let me be clear in my soul.
Let my mind not confuse me.

Let me sustain my beloved,
for you have given me this gift,

and though I know the day will come
when I must give this gift back to you,

until that day let me love him
as he loves me,

with a love that deepens my soul
and touches the abyss within me.

May we bring your presence here.
May we bring your love.

And though they may deny this love
and use it against us,

may we give them this love
in an unbroken continuum,

and though our hearts may be ripped open
and our bodies smashed and shattered

may our souls live forever in you.

XVIII

'You teach today,' he says
and all eyes fall on me.
Not all are filled with love
as they are for him, the Blessed One.

I want to pull my veil across my face
and slip away unseen.

But God is in my heart
and His words flow from my lips,
and I will always answer Him,

so I speak of the soul's rise to heaven,
breaking through each temptation,
until all that binds it has been slain
and the soul is free to be its true self,

and how we do not have to wait for death
to let our souls rise back to God,
but we can free ourselves now

to be His children, in these bodies,
to ascend to heaven while on earth,
for we are all His Blessed Ones
and He will never hurt or wound us.

Peter mutters under his breath
but I look to my beloved
and he smiles, and I remember
in God's eyes I am a Teacher, a Light,

so I let the words keep flowing,
I sing God's holy song.

So many eyes are entranced
that I speak until the sun falls,
and the women move in closer,
and the men who stay ask questions,
knowing I will have the answer.

XIX

He is always leaving me –
when the fire dims to embers
and the crowds start to gather,

when his friends call on him
to settle a debate
for which he has no time,

when they come
for healing
for rest
for peace
for hope
for faith
for love.

And yet our time together is enough,
when he takes me in his arms
and becomes that healing, rest, peace, hope, faith, love,

when he seeds them in my heart
so I may carry them within me
to give to others as he does,

for we know the day will come
when he will leave and not come back,

as we hear the cries
the wind carries across the desert
in the dying light.

XX

I was born in the waves' caress,
swept from shore to shore
needing no destination.

Now I'm stranded on dry land.
The sand burns my feet
and my throat is rasping;

and though I want to follow him,
and the pull is unforgiving,

I yearn for the sea,
its lapping lullaby,
its coolness on my breast,

my head submerged,
and my hair floating behind me
like a tangle of seaweed.

But Galilee's lullaby is long silenced,
and Jerusalem cries out for us
with a hot passion

that promises fire
and burning.

XXI

And I will love my love

until the sun goes dark,
until the seas dry up,
until the earth cracks open.

I will love my love

until the wind stops singing,
until the light burns to blackness
and the moon falls to earth.

I will love my love

until the last breath gasps from me,
until they take my lifeless body,
anoint me and bury me,

and I will still love my love

as my soul rises to his,
and we will burn as one
long after this world is gone.

XXII

He sings Hosanna
and the wind stills to listen.

It's as if he reaches into my heart
and lifts it to God,

and though my heart yearns for God
as much as his does,

I want to sing 'save us from this knowing,
change the ending.

Let us be as free as these prayers
rising to heaven.'

But I know we must play our part
before our ascent,

so I sing 'God, heal my heart
which is already breaking.'

XXIII

The road has been too long.
Now its end is nearing.

I have asked the right questions
and understood the meaning.

Yet the others stay blind
and mutter when he kisses me,

and I want to scream *can you not see
where this is leading?*

Will you not help us?

When he is on his knees
it is I who must raise him up,

to let him lean on me when he cannot walk,
to be his eyes when he only sees the darkness,

for this is my greatest love
– to help him be all he must.

I curse God for letting me
love him so deeply;

I thank God for letting me
love him so deeply.

XXIV

Mary finds me in the shadows,
pulls me close as I cry,

tells me it is strength and pain
to know something comes
that can't be fought,

that like the morning sun
he is a borrowed light
that must be given back at nightfall,

that we must be strong for him,
that our pain will flow after
and then we will have each other.

Her child will be torn from her arms
as my love will be torn from mine.

They are baying for blood
and won't be sated
until the Messiah is struck down.

But I have chosen this path.
I ask God to give me strength,

step out of the shadows
and go to him.

XXV

'I hear Him calling me,' he says.

The fire spits and crackles.
I take his hands, stroke their backs,
but still he won't look up.

'But what if I can't do all He asks of me?'

I don't ask what is asked,
but I know I must say yes
for I also hear Him calling.

'Yes you can, and you will,
for you were born to answer His call.
And I will be with you.'

'Will you stay?' he asks.
'Always.' And the promise is made
– no matter what comes I will stay.

The fire goes out and as I hold him in the dark,
I ask 'what if I can't do it?'
But before God answers, I know

I will, I must.

XXVI

And as the men pass bread,
the women pass tears.
There is no hiding now.
The dark approaches
and it won't be gone.

It wears a soldier's armour
that hides an ancient rage
that pushes against the light,
that wants to douse the fire
with its dark ash.

It can't remember it was once light
and burnt so brightly
it turned to ash,
and now it only sees
its shadow face,

and my love will do whatever it takes
to let that ash fall,
darken the earth,
feed the soil,
grow into a new tree

that will one day be cut down
and burnt again,
and this bright light,
this eternal fire
will blaze as he did

and its undying embers
will whisper his name.

XXVII

He won't let me go to him
but I watch from the shadows
as the others fall asleep.

It is time. I am not ready.
He lies prostrate on the ground,
cries to our Father 'remove this cup from me,'

and I cry 'Father, let me be with him,'
but I know I must stay,
that this moment is his alone.

I beg our Father to let him feel His presence,
to hold him in the light
as this long night falls,

for we are all falling, falling,
and by morning we will be on our knees
and the pain will only be beginning.

XXVIII

blood
          more
scourging
          more
mobs
          more
howling
          more
screaming
          more
crying
          more
no
          more
kicking
          more
falling
          more
thorns
          more
nails
          more
no
          more
God
          more
lost
          more
blood

XXIX

All I see are his feet,
his veins leaching blood,
the nails tapped tight to his skin,
the wounds opening as his knees
give in and his weight bears down,
and Mary crying for her son.

The last time I knelt
by him, I put petals red as blood
in the water I lapped over his feet,
rubbed in aloes, dried his skin,
and the way he looked at me in the fading sun
as I looked up.

But now I can't look up.
I stretch my hands towards his feet,
touch his skin
raw and burning in the sun,
and sink to my knees
in the sand caked in his blood.

I would crawl through fire on my knees
for him, tear down the sun,
rip off my skin to replace his skin
if he would only ask, but he won't look down
and I can't look up, so I scream at his feet,
and I don't know which of us is crying blood.

XXX

The sun falls

and we are left blind.
I beg our Father to lift this veil,

and then the light is in his eyes again
as he feels our Father in his heart,

and he lets the pain go.

He smiles at me
before his eyes slip shut,

and I scream on my knees,
still lost in the darkness

before the moon rises.

XXXI

I walk barefoot,
want to feel the rocks
stab my skin with every step,

to let my blood flow as his did.

I think of the night he took
my bleeding feet in his hands,
rubbed each grain of sand from my skin,
spread balm on my cuts,
wanting to heal with love, not miracles

and I wish love was enough
to create a miracle now.

I don't know which aches more,
my body or my heart,
only that the ache is all there is.

I stumble, cut my knee,
walk on. Some part of me

can still hear him calling
and answer I must.

The soldiers stop me at the tomb.
I hold up my oils.

The one who speared him
sees my bloodied feet,
orders the stone to be rolled back.

I step into the dark
to hold him one last time,
to kiss his body,
anoint his skin with myrrh and aloes
and breathe him in.

But the shroud lies limp.
I lift the bloodied linen,
fall to my knees and howl.

Even in death they take him from me.

Can I not hold him in the dark,
just me and him alone,
no one's Messiah,
no one's King,
no one's enemy.

I tear at the shroud;
his face is etched on the cloth,
flat, empty.

The darkness has hold of me
and the light can't find its way in.

I wrap his shroud around me
and lie where he lay,
in his blood thick and clumped

until my tears make it flow again,
and his blood slips around me
instead of his arms.

XXXII

I crawl from the darkness
and see a figure framed in light.

It's as if the sun burns within him,
as he calls to me.

My heart hears his song again,
and I sing back.

But I know this moment is fleeting;
he is with his true love now.

I grasp at each second
wondering which will be the last.

There is so much I should ask
but words mean nothing.

He shines so brightly
it's like looking at the heart of a star.

My eyes ache but never leave his
as his light slowly fades.

How often can I lose him
before my heart shatters?

Then I feel him stroke my face
and know he stays by my side always.

XXXIII

I will follow in the footsteps of my love
through deserts, villages and shores.

I will fulfil my promise to share his words
and speak of all he has shown me.

'God loves you, as He loves all.
Listen to your soul and let it guide you.

Let no man lead you astray from its voice
for it is the voice of God within you.

Follow it and all will flow.
Stray from it and the world of man

will pull you into its undertow.
Forgive. Shine His light.

With your presence you are His essence,
and if you walk the world as this

you will be happy, no matter what pain comes
because pain is passing but God is eternal.'

Like a bird riding the wind,
I will let God carry me.

I will show them how to follow,
and share what He whispers to me,

and on days like today
when the world is lost in darkness

and no light seems possible,
I will find the light within me.

I will take one step and then another,
and follow the tender call

of my love who still sings to me.

About the Author

Deirdre Cartmill is a Northern Irish writer. She has published two previous poetry collections, both from Lagan Press, *The Return of the Buffalo* (2013) and *Midnight Solo* (2004). She has performed widely at festivals and events across Ireland and internationally, and read at the first Muldoon's Picnic to be held outside the US. She was selected for the inaugural Irish Writers Centre Evolution Programme in 2021-22. She's previously received an Artists Career Enhancement Scheme (ACES) Award from the Arts Council of Northern Ireland. She was shortlisted for the Hennessy Literary Award and was a finalist in the Scottish International Open Poetry Competition.

She was Belfast Cathedral's Heritage Writer-in-Residence 2022-23, and has previously been Monaghan County Libraries Writer-in-Residence 2020, Irish Writers Centre Roaming Writer-in-Residence 2019, Irish Writers Centre Community Writer-in-Residence with Women's Aid 2018, and Artist-in-Residence at the Belfast International Arts Festival 2017.

She co-commissioned and co-curated Ireland's first Poetry Jukebox which is now a permanent installation in Belfast. She is also an award-winning scriptwriter. She has written for *Fair City* (RTÉ) and award-winning teen drama *Seacht* (BBC NI). Her short film *Two Little Boys* was selected for the Belfast Film Festival 2013. She was a winner of the BBC Writersroom Undercover Competition and the Claddagh Films Script Award, was a finalist in the Red Planet Prize, and has been shortlisted for many other awards. She has also written for stage and radio. Her short plays *No Paths That Are Ending* and *The Lost Souls Party* toured Northern Ireland as part of Terra Nova's Arrivals and Arrivals 2 productions. She received a seed commission from the Lyric Theatre in 2023.

Deirdre was awarded an MA with Distinction in Creative Writing from Queen's University. She has extensive experience as a creative writing mentor and facilitator, and is a part-time Lecturer in Creative Writing for Ulster University.